Original title:
The Sound of Waves

Copyright © 2025 Creative Arts Management OÜ
All rights reserved.

Author: William Hawthorne
ISBN HARDBACK: 978-1-80581-493-1
ISBN PAPERBACK: 978-1-80581-020-9
ISBN EBOOK: 978-1-80581-493-1

Embrace of Oceanic Echoes

The sea's a giggle, a playful tease,
With splashes and tickles, it's sure to please.
Crabs dance on rocks, like they're in a show,
While seagulls squawk jokes that only they know.

Waves waltz on shores, doing their twist,
They pull in the sand, but it can't resist.
Shells roll their eyes at the tide's wild spree,
Saying, 'Oh dear waves, let us be free!'

Jellyfish float like balloons on a spree,
Waving their tentacles, carefree as can be.
Each splash a chuckle, each swell a grin,
As fish join the dance, twirling with fin.

So let's grab our towels, skip worries away,
Join this ocean riddle, where silliness plays.
With laughter like bubbles, we'll frolic and dive,
In this watery world, where the giggles thrive!

Chants of the Ocean's Embrace

A sea turtle in a cape of blue,
Sings loudly, 'Oh, what shall I do?'
With seaweed as a microphone,
He claims the shore, 'I rule alone!'

Crabby sidesteps with a snappy tune,
Offering dances to the moon.
While dolphins bring their poppy cheer,
Surfing through bubbles, loud and clear.

Gusts of wind whisk puffs of foam,
As jellybeans are blown back home.
The fish form lines, they can't resist,
To groove and sway as part of the gist.

The ocean wakes, it's party time,
With sea cucumbers joining in rhyme.
When night falls and the stars all gleam,
They chant and laugh, it's quite the dream.

Melodies of the Deep

Down below, the deep notes hum,
Where squids and shrimps all have fun.
A whale conducts with a grand fin,
While bubbles float and birds swoon in.

A pufferfish, slightly puffed up,
Tried to join in, what a hiccup!
He blew a note, it went so wrong,
And scared away the little throng.

In coral groves, a concert starts,
With clinks and clanks from happy hearts.
A clam claps shells, what a show!
And a flatfish performs slow and low.

As night arrives, glowing light takes flight,
From lanternfish dancing in their delight.
The symphony of oceanic flair,
Makes even starfish sway with flair.

Serenade of the Seashore

At dawn, the gulls begin to squawk,
Telling crabs to take a walk.
Starfish start their morning chat,
While clams sing tunes, how about that?

A turtle wearing cool sunglasses,
Glides past in search of sun and jazz.
The sand castles shake with glee,
As waves say, 'Come dance with me!'

Anemones throw a foam party,
With bubble machines getting hearty.
The fish swim in rhythmic glee,
While seaweed bops like a spree.

As twilight fades, the sea yawns wide,
With dolphins putting on a slide.
The rhythm of the coast won't sleep,
For laughter echoes in the deep.

Rhythms of Water's Heart

When splashes laugh and play,
A fish decided to ballet.
He twirled with great delight,
Making seagulls take flight.

The tide rolled in, a goofy grin,
As crabs did shimmy on their fin.
An octopus in a top hat,
Sipped tea while looking for a pat.

Jellyfish threw a disco bash,
Inviting shells for a wild splash.
But one conch bopped too hard,
And now has quite the scarred regard.

The chorus of the shore sings bright,
With sea lions juggling day and night.
As waves crash down to the beat,
You can't help but tap your feet.

Frozen Notes of Liquid Dream

Penguins sliding on a frosty beam,
Chasing fish with a giggling scream.
They waddle home with fishy flair,
Cutting through the icy air.

In this land, where the snowflakes prance,
Seal pups join in a silly dance.
With icicles as shiny swords,
They boast of battles, oh the hoards!

A polar bear with shades sits tight,
Eating ice cream, what a sight!
He waves to seals, "Want some too?"
As laughter echoes, bright and blue.

Under the shimmering aurora's gleam,
Whispers of fun drift like a dream.
Frozen notes in the chilly air,
Do you hear them? Can you spare?

Cradle of the Horizon's Song

In the cradle of the foamy crest,
A walrus snores, is he impressed?
With sea anemones waving bye,
To fish that leap and almost fly.

The mermaids brush their shimmering hair,
As dolphins joke, "Do we dare?"
A clam in glasses tries to read,
While laughter blooms like ocean seed.

A pelican's on a beachside spree,
Practicing tricks for the stand-up sea.
With splashy puns and salty rhymes,
Time drifts by in the best of times.

As seabirds chirp a merry tune,
And seaglass glints beneath the moon.
Here in this place, the fun prolongs,
In the cradle of the horizon's songs!

Lullabies Drift on Salted Winds

A crab on stage forgot his hat,
Sways to the tune of a buzzing gnat.
The seashells clap with a joyful sound,
While starfish spin round and round.

An octopus juggling jellybeans,
Makes waves of laughter, bursting seams.
Seaweed shimmying like it's grand,
The narwhal leads a wacky band.

Lazy seals sunbathe with pride,
Rolling over for a bumpy ride.
While fish gossip with a splashy flair,
"Did you hear? The tide's a millionaire!"

With every ripple, joy does swell,
As barnacles share their tales to tell.
In this merry splash, we find our cheer,
With lullabies drifting, come gather near!

Shimmering Serenade in Blue

The ocean's giggle splashes wide,
Fish in bow ties take a ride.
Seagulls dance with beak in tow,
Waves are laughing, don't you know?

A crab with swagger, big and bold,
Claims a shell like it's pure gold.
While dolphins play a game of tag,
The beach ball bounces, what a brag!

Turtles race with sand in curls,
They flip for fun like little twirls.
A sunburned kid in neon gear,
Sips lemonade, let's give a cheer!

Under the sun, all troubles fade,
With salty winds, a merry parade.
So join the frolic, dance and sway,
Let's laugh it out, it's a wave-y day!

Soliloquy of the Sandy Shores

Sandy shores whisper secrets of cheer,
Tide pools giggle; their humor is clear.
A crab stands tall, wearing a hat,
Cracking jokes with a friend, and that's that!

Seagulls cackle with comic finesse,
As a sandcastle crumbles, oh what a mess!
They crow about build and take-down skills,
While tide ticks the clock; it never stands still.

A starfish jokes, 'I'm not just a five,'
'Take me to the dance, I'll truly arrive!'
The ocean replies with a splash and a roar,
Every grain of sand carries laughter galore.

And against the backdrop of sun and sea,
The shores are alive, like a grand jubilee.
With giggles and wiggles, the evening's a blast,
In this humor-filled haven, joy holds fast.

Drumbeats of the Ocean's Heart

Shells tap out rhythms on coral floors,
As crabs stage a march to the ocean's roars.
A whale plays drums with a splashy grace,
While dolphins join in with smiles on their face.

The clam gets comfortable on a rock,
And starts a beat, tick-tock, tick-tock.
But a wave rolls in, oh no, what a mess!
He flips and flops, a slippery dress!

Seagull percussionists flap their wings,
Creating chaos, oh, what fun it brings!
Fish form a conga line in a twirl,
The sea's a stage, with laughter to unfurl.

Under moonlight, the ocean plays loud,
A funny festival, making us proud.
Each wave a note, each splash a cheer,
Join the performance, it's funny down here!

Canvassed by Celestial Currents

Ocean paints its wavy art,
With splashes of laughter that tug the heart.
Pufferfish puff, like balloons on parade,
While jellyfish groove in a shimmering shade.

A clam's a comedian, pinches with glee,
Telling the octopus, 'It's all about me!'
Crabs in their shells try hard to hide,
But their ticklish toes couldn't abide.

The sea anemones wave hello,
To a school of fish trying to steal the show.
They trip on the currents, oh what a sight,
A sea of giggles from dawn until night.

From coral reefs to bright sunlit sands,
Every creature joins in the laughs and bands.
Underwater, they spread mirth like a flame,
In this wacky world, nothing's quite the same.

Symphony in Aqua Blue

The fish in tuxedos dance and twirl,
As seaweed wigs swirl and unfurl.
They do the cha-cha between the shells,
While a crab conducts with lively yells.

A dolphin giggles, flipping high,
Bubbles bursting like popcorn in the sky.
Seagulls sing off-key, what a croak,
Making merry with every joke.

A starfish tries a moonwalk sway,
Claiming it's the latest ballet.
But gets stuck on a sandy spot,
And giggles at its own new plot.

Under this show of aquatic jest,
Even the sea turtles can't rest.
They laugh so hard at the splashy scene,
This frolicsome tide is fit for a queen.

Ballad of Whispering Currents

Once there was a current, swift and sly,
Whispering secrets as it flew by.
It giggled and laughed with every twirl,
While fish sang back with a flip and a whirl.

"Oh dear me!" said a crab in a hat,
"Where's my sandwich? Did a tuna cat?"
The current just chuckled, swirling away,
While sea cucumbers planned for a play.

The starfish in chorus clapped their arms,
As playful waves flaunted their charms.
"Let's write a ballad, make it quite grand,
A tune to tickle all creatures on land!"

So the current hummed low, fast, and high,
While dolphins leaped, flinging spray to the sky.
With a friendly wink, they sang through the night,
In a seaside ballad, oh what a sight!

Lyrics of the Glistening Waters

In the glistening pool, a frog in a hat,
Crows out his lyrics—imagine that!
He strums on a kelp, all slimy and green,
While fish hold a concert, a curious scene.

With a splash here and there, they try to take part,
Each trying to sing from the bottom of their heart.
A crab plays maracas, all clickety-clack,
Even octopuses boogie, don't hold them back!

A clam beats the drums, quite the show,
While eels do the cha-cha, to and fro.
The water sparkles, laughter in waves,
As funny fish tales the ocean braves.

So join in the fun, let's sing with glee,
Under the sun, by the happy sea.
For there's music aplenty, in every splash,
With tunes of the waters, a whimsical bash!

Songbird by the Sea

A songbird sings on a rocky shore,
With a squawk that sounds like a booming roar.
It taps its feet on the driftwood log,
While crabs dance along in a silly fog.

Oh, the jellyfish join in the fun,
With wobbly jigs, they sway and run.
While starfish giggle, stuck to a stone,
The songbird croons, never alone.

From sunrise soft to the sunset bright,
It sings of seaweed and fish in flight.
A flip-flop splash, a wiggly twist,
Who knew fish had a beat? Who could resist?

So here's to the bird, our comical friend,
Whose laughter and song can never end.
From coast to coast, hear that cheerful tune,
Dancing with waves beneath the moon.

Nautical Nightingale

A bird perched high, what a sight,
With a hat made from seaweed, oh so tight!
It squawks at boats like a captain grand,
Chasing after fish that got out of hand.

The seagulls cheer, they sing along,
To the tune of splashes, where they belong.
The fish roll their eyes, swim far away,
From the loudest bird on a sunny day.

When the tide comes up, it steers the tale,
A madcap melody that'll never pale.
It flaps and flutters, creating a fuss,
While dolphins laugh, ride the ocean bus.

So if you hear that rambunctious tune,
Know it's our bird, under the moon.
With feathers of gold and a voice full of zest,
Nautical Nightingale, you are the best!

Tales Carried by the Current

The river giggles as it plays along,
Juggling pebbles like a moving song.
Frogs in bowties leap with finesse,
Hopping and bopping in water's dress.

With tales of fish riding on the wind,
They make the bravest little fish grinned.
A turtle rushes, but oh my dear,
Trips on a lily, what a silly smear!

Whispers travel from stream to sea,
Sharing secrets just like you and me.
With waves of laughter and merry cheer,
Every flow captures a whimsical sphere!

As the sun sets, reflections play,
The current sings, is this a holiday?
With stories twirling, laughter so bright,
We leave with smiles, all feeling light!

Cadence of the Ever-Swaying Sea

The ocean dips low, then pops back high,
Bubbles bounce up, waving goodbye.
Fish in tuxedos swim with flair,
While surfing seals chill without a care.

We watch a whale do a belly flop,
The splash is so loud, we all want to stop.
Seagulls perform their acrobatic shows,
While crabs take bets on their comedy prose!

Splashing around, what a joyful sound,
Every wave dances, each tide is profound.
Seashells are gossiping, tongues wagging fast,
About the beach party that was a blast!

The sea can be silly, playful, and bright,
Filling our hearts with laughter and light.
With drifts of seaweed that tickle our toes,
We leave the shoreline, but the fun still grows!

Murmurs in the Sand

Footprints wander, then fade away,
As the gulls squawk and dance in play.
A dog plays fetch, but oh dear me!
He brings back a fish, not the ball, you see.

The waves make whispers, soft and sweet,
Tickling toes, a gentle treat.
Sandy sandwiches, not quite right,
With a side of salt and a splash of delight!

A crab with a hat scuttles on by,
Waving hello with a wink in his eye.
Forget the lunch, it's a beach party!
With every wave, it's chaos so hearty!

Seashells giggle as they find a mate,
While the sun slips down—it's getting late.
With stories of laughter, the shore takes a bow,
Who knew sand could be so fun right now?

Lullaby of the Coastal Breeze

Little crabs dance on the shore,
Hiding from seagulls, wanting more.
Sandcastles tumble as the tide creeps,
While winy shells giggle in deep sleeps.

With jellyfish wiggling, a silly sight,
They float like balloons in the soft moonlight.
Giggles of fish in a splashy spree,
Underwater twirls, oh so carefree!

The breeze whispers secrets, oh so grand,
As flip-flops flop on the hot, wet sand.
Children's laughter, a bubbly tune,
Echoes around like a merry balloon!

Even the seashells chuckle aloud,
With every wave, they're so very proud.
While crabs make jokes and chase with glee,
Can you believe this shenanigan spree?

Tranquil Splash at Dusk

With a wink and a splash, the waves set the pace,
Fish flip-flopped in a comical race.
A clam told jokes that made us snort,
While octopuses played tic-tac-sport.

The sunset glowed in a cotton candy sky,
As crabs in tuxedos shuffled by.
They showcased moves from a Broadway hit,
While jellyfish cheered, 'Don't you quit!'

Bubbles floated like thoughts in a haze,
The sea chuckled softly, lost in a daze.
A message in a bottle rolled in to shore,
'Have a laugh and come back for more!'

So dance with the currents, splash in delight,
Find joy in each wave, and hold on tight.
For in this playful sea of jest,
Every moment is hilariously blessed!

Interlude of Misty Horizons

At dusk the seagulls took a break,
To sip their tea and eat some cake.
While fishermen fished for a silly thrill,
Complaining of the tides and chill.

A crab announced his silly dance,
Waving claws, he took his chance.
The fishy crowd applauded loud,
As clouds rolled by, a fluffy crowd.

A starfish tried to start a band,
But only got the sand in hand.
They strummed on shells with utmost glee,
The ocean shook, 'What's wrong with me?'

So join the laughter, join the fun,
With flip-flops flapping, out in the sun.
We revel in waves, and join the tale,
Where every splash is a silly sail!

Tidal Echoes in the Mist

In foggy coats, the dolphins play,
Making jokes in their silly way.
A whale chimed in with a deep bass note,
While swimmers wondered, 'Who's the goat?'

The mist rolled in with a cozy grin,
As pirates claimed, 'Let the fun begin!'
A treasure map? Just jellybeans,
And mermaids giggled from sandy scenes.

Each wave a plot twist, grand and bold,
Fishermen laughed, their stories told.
With bait in hand, they cast away,
Chasing dreams, come what may!

As laughter echoed on every swell,
The sea's own joke, a frothy spell.
In this misty place of playful cheer,
We find our voices, loud and clear!

Voice of the Horizon's Horizon

While surfing on a tuna's back,
I lost my snack, oh what a whack.
Seagulls laughed with fishy glee,
As waves danced with a cup of tea.

A crab in shades took a sunlit pause,
Claiming the surf, without a cause.
I bobbed around, a beach ball in flight,
With flip-flops slapping, what a sight!

A dolphin called, 'Hey, join my band!'
But I just splashed, thinking I'd planned.
They sang of tides, I laughed in pie,
Oh fishy tales, they never lie!

So here's to waves, and laughter bright,
An ocean tale, a silly sight.
With frothy friends and sandy feet,
We dance to rhythms, oh so sweet!

Elysian Tones of Ocean Breeze

The breeze blew softly with a cheeky grin,
As surfers collided, fish roared in.
My beach ball rose like it had a mind,
Then down it went, leaving me behind.

A crab in a tutu took quite a bow,
I clapped too loud, had to take a vow.
Seashells giggled as they rolled along,
With echoes of laughter, our hearts felt strong.

Saltwater tickles and whimsy abound,
With each silly wave, joy can be found.
We danced on the shore, in costumes so wild,
Every tide brought fun, like a giddy child.

Rhythms of the Soughing Sea

The ocean's rhythm is quite a blast,
While jellyfish dance, I quickly passed.
A surfboard crash like a clown's big fall,
As waves keep rolling, I'm giving my all.

A fish in a tux, really stole the scene,
With bubbles of laughter, things turned green.
My snorkel fogged up, I missed the fun,
Giggling dolphins, just look how they run!

Splashes of humor, with tides that tease,
Seashell jokes, a truly silly breeze.
We rocked the boat, amidst laughter's roar,
Who knew the sea was a stand-up store?

Waves of Wanderlust

My flip-flops flew, just like a kite,
Chasing a crab that gave me a fright.
Sailing the sea, I found a fish,
Wearing a hat, oh what a wish!

A sailor's hat upon my head,
I tripped on the deck and fell like lead.
The fish winked at me, oh how absurd,
With bubbles popping, it simply stirred.

The tide pulled me in, a playful tease,
While gulls dive-bombed, aiming to please.
We laughed with splashes, a water ballet,
In this frolicking sand, we'd happily stay!

Nautical Narratives in Echoes

A seagull stole my sandwich, oh dear,
It squawked with glee, as I shed a tear.
The boat rocked gently, a comic show,
As I searched for snacks it couldn't bestow.

The captain danced, a jig on the deck,
Trip over a barrel, what the heck?
Fish leaped, laughing at our mischief,
While crew mates shouted, 'Give it a whiff!'

A lobster wearing shades caught my eye,
Sipping on soda, without a shy.
The ocean chuckled, waves like friends,
As laughter echoed, our fun never ends.

Melody in the Misty Dawn

A foggy morning with a curious gleam,
The waves whisper secrets, like a morning dream.
Paddling penguins form a goofy parade,
As suns and seas mingle, laughter's displayed.

Footprints in sand lead us to frolic,
While jellyfish bob in a dance so ironic.
The sea's gentle rhythm serenades the day,
While clashing surf sends sandcastles away.

Mermaids giggle, their hair in a toss,
As dolphins leap by, they never seem lost.
The morning becomes a hilarious show,
As I trip on a wave and down I do go!

In this mist, the humor flows like the tide,
Each wave brings a smile I cannot abide.
With coral-shaped laughter, serenity calls,
In this melodic dawn, joy gracefully sprawls!

Oceanic Overture of Peace

The sun's halo shines on the rippling spray,
As dolphins dance in a spirited play.
They flip and they flounder, a sight to behold,
Making waves with laughter, pure joy uncontrolled.

Beach balls zoom through the salty sea breeze,
With splashes and giggles, our worries do ease.
An octopus juggles both shells and a star,
While I try to balance—it's comedic by far.

Flip-flops fly as we race to the shore,
Making puddles that splash, while we clamour for more.
The jellyfish wobbles in a whimsical sway,
While crabs do the moonwalk, it's all in the play.

With umbrellas upturned and sunscreen amiss,
We embrace every chaos, nothing's amiss.
A symphony here that's light, kind, and fun,
In this oceanic overture, laughter has won!

Symphony of the Roaring Tide

The ocean roars in a comical way,
Sirens singing tunes of the silly bay.
Fish in tuxedos swim by in a rush,
While waves give us a bubbly, frothy hush.

Bottles bobbing with secrets untold,
We'll find a treasure that's worth more than gold.
A crab in my flip-flop offers to dance,
I throw it back in, I missed my chance!

The surf's a stage, with a splash and a crash,
Seashells tap dance while we drop and we splash.
Our laughter echoes beneath the blue sky,
As seaweed wigs wave hello and goodbye.

In this watery concert, we giggle and shout,
Making friends with the tide, we wander about.
Each wave a note in a joyful parade,
A riotous symphony, mermaids invade!

Crescendo of the Cresting Waves

The seagulls squawk, oh what a show,
As they dive for snacks, but rarely go slow.
With every splash and every shout,
I wonder what this fuss is about.

Sandcastles fall with a comical plunk,
A toddler's gleam, then a tidal trunk.
Buckets fly as the tide rolls back,
We laugh and swim, avoiding the whack.

Crabs scuttle sideways, in a fashion so spry,
While I chase my hat that's now soaring high.
The waves crash down with a bubbly cheer,
Our beach day antics bring endless mirth here.

As the sun sets low, we can't quite depart,
With salty laughter that fills up the heart.
The ocean's giggles dance with the night,
Waving goodbye, what a hilarious sight!

Tidal Celebrations of Serenity

In puddles of joy, we skipped along,
As snappy sea snails hummed a snazzy song.
With crabs wearing hats and a seaweed tie,
We laughed as seagulls tried to fly high.

The foam did a jig on the sandy shore,
And shells clinked together like friends wanting more.
A mischievous wave gave a cheeky wink,
While beachgoers chuckled, forgetting to think.

Kites danced above, fluttering bold,
As a fish in sunglasses attempted to scold.
The sun flipped pancakes on this magical day,
While jellybeans floated, sweet sorcery at play.

With tide pools like mirrors reflecting our glee,
We celebrated nature with giggles so free.
Each splash was a story, laughter the theme,
In the tides of life where we all dared to dream.

Undercurrent of Forgotten Songs

Under the waves where the mermaids sing,
A clam called out for the latest bling.
With pearls in hand and bubbles galore,
Seashells held concerts that left me in awe.

An octopus juggled while saying, 'Hey, look!'
'This seaweed's a hit in my cookbook!'
The crab did the cha-cha, so spry and spruced,
As fish lined up, their tails deduced.

Seahorses pranced with an elegant flair,
But then tripped and tumbled in saltwater air.
Their laughter echoed through coral and foam,
In the playful abyss, all felt at home.

A bubble floated by with a giggling tone,
Sampling the flavors of the salty unknown.
With tides that roared and whispers that hummed,
Life under the sea was perfectly fun.

Fluid Whispers at Twilight

The sun bowed down, all golden and bright,
As fish in tuxedos swam left and right.
Oysters giggled, pearls escaped their grip,
While dolphins joined in with a flip and slip.

The tide sucked in my favorite hat,
And whales swayed side to side, imagine that!
As the moon played peek-a-boo with the sea,
I laughed at the waves, 'Come paddle with me!'

Barnacles wiggled, thinking they could dance,
And crabs formed a line; how could I miss the chance?
With slight-of-hand tricks, they caught a fish,
As gulls barked laughter, granting my wish.

The night hummed softly, salty and sweet,
Every splash declared a comedic feat.
Shells whispered secrets, giggles so bright,
In this twilight of folly, all felt just right.

Cadence of the Crashing Surf

A seagull danced on my ice cream cone,
With a laugh that made the children groan.
The ocean splashed, it wore a grin,
As it tickled toes that dared to swim.

My hat flew off, chased by the tide,
While crabs marched on, with a comical pride.
Flip-flops flying, laughter in the air,
A beach party where no one has a care.

A jellyfish bounced like a silly toy,
It wobbled past, causing glee and joy.
Sneaky waves played peek-a-boo,
Splashing shirts and socks—oh, who knew?

Sandcastles crumbled; kids wore frowns,
But then, surfboards painted in clowns.
With each sea giggle and bubbly shout,
We danced on the shore, no room for doubt.

Lullabies of the Shoreline's Embrace

The lull of the tide sings low and sweet,
As sandpipers tap, with tiny feet.
A whale off in the distance made a joke,
While crabs in the shallows giggled and spoke.

Mermaids painted seashell nails so bright,
As dolphins danced under the silver light.
Starfish had a party, all in a row,
With giggles and gags, stealing the show.

The driftwood dreamed of sailing afar,
While sea cucumbers showed off their scar.
The clattering waves stacked pebbles with flair,
As laughter echoed through the salty air.

So find your joy at the water's edge,
Where silliness reigns, we all make a pledge.
With lullabies of laughter and waves that gleam,
The shorelines embrace us, together we dream!

Rhythms of the Rolling Surf

The surf rolls in with a dance so bright,
Waves high five seagulls taking flight.
A sandy dog runs with joyous pride,
Chasing his tail, he can't help but glide.

The foam did tickle a toddler's toes,
As sandcastles giggled, "Here we go!"
The beach ball bounced like it was alive,
While the tide played tag, oh what a dive!

Shells were the audience, listening keen,
To every silly trick, every scene.
A crab with a hat, posed for a pic,
While the waves chuckled, doing a flick.

So join the fun where the ocean beams,
In the splash and the frolic, we chase our dreams.
With rhythms of laughter, we find our glee,
In the crazy, joyful, sandy spree!

Murmurs from the Ocean Depths

Bubbles giggle like a child at play,
As the octopus sketched in murky gray.
Anemones swayed to a jazzy tune,
While the sharks rolled their eyes, oh how they'd swoon!

Crabs donned sunglasses, striking a pose,
As the seaweed twirled in elegant flows.
Fish did a conga, each one a clown,
In the colorful depths, nobody frowns.

A turtle played solo on a seashell drum,
While the shrimp beat time, they loved the strum.
Comedic mariners in the sunlit wave,
Splashing and laughing, so bold and brave.

So let's hear the chuckles from below,
In this underwater show, watch it glow.
With humor and laughter, the ocean's delight,
Making waves of giggles, oh what a sight!

Serenade of the Swelling Sea

In the splash of a seagull's cry,
The fish make faces as they fly.
A crab did a tap dance on the sand,
While the waves giggled, oh so grand.

A clam played hide and seek with me,
Wiggling sideways like it was free.
The frothy foam tossed a silly hat,
As dolphins took a bow, imagine that!

Coconuts rolled like soccer balls,
Seashells whispered the sea's best calls.
A jellyfish waved with a jelly-like laugh,
While starfish argued about their own half.

So here we dance, on this sandy scene,
Where the sea's a circus, wild and clean.
With whispers and giggles, we cheer and play,
In the great jest of life, come what may.

Navigator's Hymn of the Sea

A sailor sings of a perilous plight,
Chasing seagulls that take their flight.
The compass spins as he stumbles and sways,
While fish eye him, with bemused gaze.

His hat flies off; it's a comical scene,
Floating away like a restive dream.
The waves giggle, tickle his toes,
Cackling at antics no one quite knows.

They sail by boats made of jelly and cream,
While pirates grapple with laughter's theme.
Shouting "Arrr!" with a joyful zest,
They keep their treasure in a funny quest!

So come aboard this whimsical ride,
With winds of mirth and hearts open wide.
The sea, a stage where we all play,
In a navigator's hymn, come what may!

Starlit Chorus of the Waves

Stars above in a giggling mood,
Watch the beach bum's funny brood.
Tidal waves crashing like a joke,
As sand squirts back, they just poke!

A dolphin pops with a gleeful splash,
Tickling surfers, what a bash!
Seashells chuckle in a line,
Ticking off names like a comic sign.

Moonlit shadows playtag on the shore,
While crabs declare, 'We want more!'
A shimmering fish sings off-key,
As seagulls shimmy to the melody.

With laughter woven in night's embrace,
Galactic giggles in every space.
The ocean whispers a cheeky tune,
Under the gaze of a sleepy moon.

Beachfront Ballads of Forgotten Times

Once a crab wore a tiny hat,
Pretending like he was the big brat.
He started a band with shells and sand,
Their tunes? A bit out of hand!

Old flip-flops singing to the tide,
Grumpy seashells take it in stride.
The starfish clapped with glee and grace,
While jellyfish paused to join the race.

Toasty sunbathers share their snacks,
With squirrels on surfboards doing acts.
The tide rolls in with comic flair,
As laughter echoes everywhere!

So let's remember the songs of yore,
The funny tales from the ocean's floor.
With every wave and sandy rhyme,
We dance to the rhythm of happy time!

Shores of Celestial Harmony

Seagulls dance like silly fools,
Wearing shades and acting cool.
They steal fries, oh what a sight,
While crabs just laugh, it feels so right.

The horizon winks at the suns,
As waves play tug-of-war for fun.
A beach ball gets caught in a breeze,
Rolling away, oh how it teases!

Children shriek while splashing about,
The lifeguard's face, a constant pout.
An ice cream truck rings chimes with glee,
While sandcastles melt like silly tea!

Here on shores of blissful jest,
Laughter floats, this place is the best.
With every splash and joyful cheer,
We find our hearts just feel sincere.

Crests of Crystal Moonlight

Beneath the shiny moonlight,
The waves all start to wink,
As sneaky tides take selfies,
And skies begin to link.

Stars twinkle with a chuckle,
As fish throw secret sparks,
Dancing with the moonbeams,
Toying 'round with the sharks.

A hermit crab in pajamas,
Claps wildly on the shore,
While the ocean hums a tune,
That begs for just one more.

In this nightly gala,
With surf as merry guest,
The laughter of the ocean,
Makes bedtime quite a jest.

Song of the Raging Tempest

The clouds are twirling wildly,
Like dancers out of tune,
Rain drops tap like jazz bands,
As thunder sings a croon.

An octopus plays maracas,
While fish jump in a line,
And turtles roll their shells,
Like music made of brine.

The winds begin to whisper,
With giggles low and sly,
As waves conspire in secret,
To give the sky a try.

A dolphin with a kazoo,
Keeps rhythm on the go,
While crabs keep time with claws,
In this water ballet show.

Ballad of the Breaking Foam

Oh! The bubbly ocean,
With froth upon its lips,
Invites the seagulls over,
For some rude dancing flips.

A starfish stuck on the shore,
Screams, 'Help! I'm in a bind!'
While oysters giggle softly,
At mischief left behind.

Splashing friends are grinning,
From puddles to a splash,
Except for one poor fella,
Who's faceplanted—what a crash!

With surfboards shaped like doughnuts,
They ride the wavy crest,
While crabs host a wild party,
And clam shells are the best.

Harmonies of Shore and Surf

Seagulls squawk with glee,
Tumbling like a clown,
Fish dance in the ocean,
While crabs boogie down.

Sandy toes are ticklish,
With seaweed in your hair,
A jellyfish did wave hello,
But yikes! It's hard to bear!

Flip-flops fly like rockets,
Feet sprinting with the tide,
You chase a sneaky wavelet,
Then find it's gone to hide!

The sun's a blazing joker,
It makes us all so bright,
As laughter fills the coastline,
In pure daydream delight.

Odes to the Ocean's Serengeti

In the realm of the waves where the critters collide,
A whale burst forth, just trying to glide.
She flipped and she flopped, made a flip-flop sound,
While everyone watched from their spots on the ground.

A seal slid by with a rock on its nose,
"Hey! I'm a clown!" it bellowed, clever prose.
The fish nearby rolled, caught in a fit,
While barnacles clapped, hey, they can't quit!

Tidal pools sparkled with laughter galore,
As shrimp threw a party, they danced on the floor.
The waves did the cha-cha, a rhythmic affair,
With sand as the dance floor, they twirled everywhere!

So stand on the shore, see the oceanous show,
With every big splash, let the giggles just flow.
For in this vast setting, so fun and so free,
The ocean's a circus, come on and see!

Refractions in the Salt-Kissed Air

The sun hit the waves with a dazzling wink,
While fish played cards, who'd have thought? Don't blink!
They'd bet on seaweed, gleaming and green,
While a sea turtle judged, quite the serene.

Jellyfish floated with grace and finesse,
Dodging the gulls who were looking for mess.
The tide rolled in, giggling like a child,
As the crabs waved goodbye, looking quite wild.

An octopus flipped pancakes on the sand,
While kids built castles, oh so grand.
But with each big wave came a giggle and splash,
Wiping the smiles, then the laughter would crash.

So when you're out where the sea meets the sky,
Remember the antics, the reason to fly.
With surfboards and laughter, come take a dare,
For in the bright ocean, all's fun if you care!

Songs of the Wind-Swept Coast

The wind whistled tunes through a hole in a rock,
While gulls played tag with a seaweed sock.
Crabs in the sand were plotting their pranks,
Donning tiny hats, making silly ranks.

A dolphin leapt with an acrobatic flair,
Diving through jokes that floated on air.
While waves rolled by, tickling toes,
A clam shouted, "Hey! Where'd my lunch go?"

Beach balls bounced with a giggling glee,
While umbrellas danced, wild and free.
The sun laughed bright, casting playful rays,
As surfboards rode bright, wavy arrays.

So tune in to laugh where the wind sings loud,
Join the cheeky fun, be part of the crowd.
With a splash and a giggle, the coast makes its call,
In such silly moments, we can all have a ball!

Cadence of the Ebb and Flow

The tide rolled in with a playful grin,
A crab danced sideways, what a silly win!
Seagulls squawked like they knew the joke,
As beachgoers slipped on a wayward soak.

A shell named Fred thought he'd sing along,
But only hummed out a funny song.
The surf said "Hey! Join in and splash!"
And suddenly Fred became quite the bash!

The fish below giggled, what a sight!
Flipping and flopping in sheer delight.
The breeze chimed in, a breeze full of cheer,
Waving at sandcastles, drawing them near.

So next time you hear a bubbly cheer,
Remember the waves love a laugh, my dear!
Join in the fun, let the rhythm sway,
Who knew that the ocean could play all day?

Tales Carried by the Ocean's Breath

A fisherman sets sail,
With tall tales to regale,
But the fish just roll their eyes,
As stories turn to lies.

A beach ball takes its flight,
Out of reach, what a sight,
It bounces, rolls, then floats,
While kids chase like lost goats.

Underneath the sun's glance,
Crabs perform a quick dance,
With one catchin' all the flak,
From his buddy's silly quack.

As day fades into night,
The sea glimmers, oh so bright,
Whispers of funny lore,
Tales of laughter by the shore.

Pastoral Phrases of the Beach

Sandcastles stand so proud,
A sandy royal crowd,
But when the waves roll high,
They wave their grand goodbye.

A picnic gone awry,
With sandwiches that fly,
As gulls swoop in and dive,
To claim that lunch alive.

Children chase the tides,
In their wild, joyful rides,
But oops! A wave sneaks in,
And the chase must begin again.

With each wave's retreat,
The beach holds rhythms sweet,
As laughter fills the air,
Nature's funny affair.

Chords from the Rocky Inlet

A tide pool's concert starts,
With seaweed strumming arts,
Starfish tapping their limbs,
While mussels hum in hymns.

Along the rocky tract,
A seal gives quite the act,
He's juggling with a fish,
An odd but funny wish.

Seagulls gather for a show,
Joining in with squeaks and crow,
They squawk, they dive, they land,
In a splashy, comic band.

When waves begin to play,
They dance the frothy ballet,
With laughter and a cheer,
Seashells wave back, sincere.

Tides of Tranquil Resonance

In the quiet afternoon,
Seagulls caw and swoon,
A crab's got quite the gait,
But it's really just late.

Children splash and shout,
Their laughter leaves no doubt,
That wet socks are the game,
Yet they still feel no shame.

A clam tries to keep pace,
With all the leaping grace,
It wiggles, wiggles strong,
But the tide just sings along.

As waves tickle the shore,
We wonder, could there be more?
An octopus in disguise,
Pokes fun with curious eyes.

Dance of the Water's Edge

The surf waltzes back with flair,
Tickling toes of the passersby.
Ocean spray forms a misty veil,
As beach balls bounce in the sky.

A flip-flop launches with glee,
It lands safely on a sunburned toe.
The tide closes in for a hug,
"Hey buddy, not so close, whoa!"

A sandcastle falls with a thud,
While giggles erupt from a child.
The ocean hums a soft tune,
As footprints wash away, reviled.

Life's a dance at the water's edge,
With splashy cha-chas all around.
Even the clams join in the fun,
In a rhythm that knows no bound!

The Whispering Reef

Bubbles rise with a giggle,
Coral sways in a silly dance.
A sea turtle sings off-key,
Chasing fish in a haphazard prance.

Starfish lounge, looking quite chill,
Their five arms fully extended.
An octopus grins with a wink,
His charm's always recommended.

The snorkeling crew strikes a pose,
Underwater selfies abound.
Giggling fish give thumbs up,
Making sure smiles are profound.

With each wave comes a belly flop,
And laughter echoes all around.
Who knew the ocean had jokes?
In the deep, fun is always found!

Ballad of the Salt and Surf

The beach is buzzing with cheer,
Kids building castles so grand.
Seagulls eye my ice cream cone,
I might need a bodyguard band.

I think I spotted a shark,
Turns out it's just a flip flop.
But wait, what's that on my arm?
A crab that just won't stop.

Tides come in, and I lose my hat,
It sails like a ship on its quest.
The sun beats down, I must admit,
Sitting still is a welcome rest.

Old men fish with jokes so dry,
While surfboards take flight and flip.
If laughter's the best medicine,
I'd say shore life is quite the trip!

Whirl of the Wandering Currents

Sea foam tickles my toes,
As seagulls steal fries from my plate.
The tide pulls back in a rush,
Crabs dance like they're late for a date.

Splashing now seems like a race,
While I wobble, trying to stand.
A dolphin leaps in my dreams,
Or maybe it's just the sand.

Waves whisper jokes to the shore,
I chuckle at seaweed's bad hair.
Fish swim by with little hats,
I can't help but stop and stare.

A shell offers me its advice,
Says to chill out and just float.
I dive under, then pop back up,
Who knew sea life could be a hoot?

Reflections of the Timeless Tide

Mirrors of water, where fish pull pranks,
While barnacles giggle in seashell banks.
An eel with a wig claims he's Debutante,
Sashaying around, a watery font.

The waves tickle toes and splash the crowd,
While sea turtles cheer, they laugh out loud.
A starfish comedian tells cosmic jokes,
Making all the sea critters giggle and poke.

The Pulse of Distant Shores

Beats of laughter across the bay,
As dolphins dance in a water ballet.
A clam in a tux, so sharply dressed,
Claims he's the star of this beachy fest.

With each wave a giggle, a splish-splash song,
Urging all the sea creatures to sing along.
The fish throw confetti, what a sight,
Celebrating moonbeams through the night.

Rhapsody of the Whispering Coast

The shores giggle as tides come in,
Their secret chuckles and playful din.
Seagulls swoop with comic grace,
Chasing shadows in a silly race.

A conch shell whispers silly tales,
Of fish in tuxedos sailing gales.
The sandpipers join in with a drum,
Marching to rhythms, feeling so numb.

Dune's Dream of Space

A sandy hill in cosmic plight,
Where grains of joy take wondrous flight.
A starfish beams with glowing glee,
Singing karaoke to a seaweed tree.

The crabs all dance, they twist and twirl,
While jellyfish get dizzy in a whirl.
An octopus juggles shells with flair,
As moonlit laughter fills the air.

Harmonies Beneath the Moonlit Tide

The moon beams down like a giant lamp,
On sandcastles that got lost in the damp.
Crickets chirp jokes, make the night light,
While waves tickle the land, a playful sight.

The stars above laugh at the sea's witty ways,
As fish start a conga, they're in a craze!
With every splash, nature's own band,
Making music through grains of the soft, wet sand.

Symphonies from the Shimmering Shore

The conch shell blows a farting sound,
Echoing laughter all around.
Each wave claps hands, making a scene,
While a fish twirls like a ballerine.

A sunburnt tourist, in panic, will run,
From a wave that's plotting to have some fun!
Shells do a dance, in a circular line,
Underneath the sun, all feeling divine.

Echoes of the Tidal Dance

Waves whisper jokes in a bubbly tone,
They tickle the toes, then they moan!
Each splash a punchline, laughter galore,
Even the starfish are rolling on the shore.

The dolphins leap like they're on a spree,
Chasing their tails, oh so carefree!
The seaweed sways in a funny hat,
While crabs do a jig, imagine that!

Whispers of the Coastal Breeze

Seagulls squawk in silly flights,
Their sandwiches stolen, what a sight!
The ocean laughs, splashes of foam,
As crabs do the cha-cha, far from home.

A jellyfish wobbles, trying to glide,
With a bow tie on, it swings with pride!
The beach ball bounces, runs from the tide,
While kids just giggle, and play as they ride.

Secrets in the Swell

The tide whispers secrets, a fishy delight,
With clam gossip shared under moon's soft light.
Shells start a rumor about the seafoam,
As turtles tell tales of their quest for a home.

An anchor's forgotten, it's spinning around,
While whales beatbox, creating a sound.
The sand tickles toes, with a cheeky grin,
As the ocean beams wide, letting fun times begin.

Dances of Deep Blue

Octopus ballet with a splashy flair,
Jellyfish giggling, floating in air.
The mollusks all cheer with a hearty trill,
As dolphins do cartwheels, showing their skill.

Squid wear bow ties and practice their spin,
While clowns of the reef start a raucous din.
Starfish suggest a conga line dance,
As sea urchins wobble, losing their chance.

Maritime Echoes of Solitude

A lone boat sways, lost in a dream,
The captain's asleep, or so it would seem.
Pelicans roll their eyes in disdain,
As barnacles laugh on the old, rusty chain.

Waves throw their jokes, a splash here and there,
Tickling the fisherman's messy, wild hair.
"Catch me if you can!" a seagull will squawk,
As otters hold hands and begin to rock.

Timeless Tide's Embrace

The ocean tickles toes, oh what a tease,
Crabs in tuxedos dance with the breeze.
Seagulls plot with snappy remarks,
While fish play disco, leaving little sparks.

The buoy's off-key song is quite a show,
Waves clap their hands, putting on a glow.
Old driftwood chuckles, the shore's best friend,
As starfish giggle, pretending to spend.

Ballad of the Restless Seafoam

Seafoam giggles as it rolls ashore,
Playing tag with toes that soar.
"Splash me lightly, don't you dare!"
It whispers mischief in the air!

A whale in sunglasses swims on by,
With a flip and a wink, oh my, oh my!
Crabs do cartwheels, it's quite a sight,
Under the sun, everything feels right!

A buoy sings with rusted cheer,
Making friends with clouds so near.
Fish parade with bubbles bright,
Their midday frolic brings pure delight!

Tides will shift, and tales will weave,
In this land where we believe.
Life's a joke with a salty grin,
Every splash, our laughter to win!

Reflections on the Liquid Canvas

Waves paint stories on the shore,
Laughing like children, wanting more.
A surfboard glides with joyous flair,
As fishy friends glance, unaware!

Seagulls squawk, "Hey, that's my snack!"
As beach balls bounce in a joyful whack.
Sandcastles rise in regal style,
Then crash down with a comical smile!

Umbrellas dance in the summer breeze,
While sunscreen fights its slippery tease.
Sand between toes, oh what a plight,
If laughter's the goal, we're rich tonight!

Watermelon slices, sunburned cheeks,
All join together for giggly peaks.
The ocean laughs with all its might,
While we sing songs 'til the fading light.

Melodies of the Crashing Breakers

The ocean's voice is filled with glee,
As shells discuss their destiny.
Crabs wearing hats and dancing shoes,
Join the party, they can't refuse!

A fish named Fred sings off key,
And seaweed joins in harmony.
Starfish clap with eight-fingered cheer,
While mermaids roll their eyes in fear!

Surfers tumble, land on their backs,
Making waves with comic cracks.
The tide's a jester, ever so merry,
With sea foam whipped like sugary dairy!

Creating laughs with frothy spray,
Seashells chime, come join the play.
Ocean's song, a funny delight,
Makes us chuckle from day to night.

Chants of the Endless Horizon

When the ocean hums a tune,
Seagulls dance and catch a swoon.
A crab in shades, he's quite the sight,
Dancing sideways, what a delight!

Fishermen sing with fishy breath,
Casting nets like poets' death.
Bubbles rise like jokes untold,
Under the sun, they shimmer bold!

Surfboards zoom, they've got some flair,
Riding waves like they just don't care.
Watch the splash when surfers fall,
They laugh it off, they're having a ball!

In the distance, a boat goes 'whoosh!'
While dolphins giggle, make a push.
Joy and chaos, it's quite a show,
Life is best when waves can flow.

Echoes Beneath the Surface

Beneath these blue waves, the fish hold court,
Telling jokes about shrimps with a frothy report.
A splash of a fin, and giggles ensue,
Like playful mariners sailing right through.

Echoing laughter, so merry and light,
As barnacles dance under the moonlight.
An octopus juggles, tentacles all,
In the laughter-filled depths, we're having a ball!

Whispers of the Tides

Amongst sandy castles, a king crab prance,
Whispers in shells hold the ocean's dance.
Waves tickle the shore, a playful retreat,
The sand tickles toes, oh, what a treat!

Each bubble that bursts shares a giggling tale,
While dolphins in shadows decorate the trail.
A conch shell, they say, can help you hear,
The punchlines of life from far and near.

Woven Melodies of the Coastal Horizon.

The ocean's a DJ, spinning tunes all day,
With beats from the surf, it makes me sway.
The crabs join the chorus, pinch to the groove,
While the fish in the deep do the funky move.

Bubbles pop like popcorn, a salty delight,
Seashells are trumpets, oh what a sight!
Wave upon wave, they're singing a song,
I can't help but laugh, floating right along.

Soundscapes of the Shifting Sands

As the tide rolls in, my flip-flops flee,
Each wave is a chuckle, they laugh at me.
Seagulls squawk jokes, their beaks filled with sand,
I wave back in style, with a splashing hand.

My towel's a sail, caught in the breeze,
It flips and it flops, with ultimate ease.
I dive for a shell, but it's just a snack,
The ocean keeps giggling, never looking back.

Shadows Beneath the Nautical Sky

Bubbles arose from a deep-sea clown,
Whose jokes made the fish all giggle and drown.
With fins a-flap and scales all aglow,
His antics and puns swept the sea floor below!

A whale tried to sing though his voice cracked bad,
While seagulls hooted; it wasn't so sad.
The starfish winked, giving a thumbs up,
As a sea turtle joined in for a chummy cup!

The sun dipped low, turning shadows to dance,
Crabs doing splits made a daring prance.
The ocean erupted in giggles and roars,
Beneath the nautical sky—oh, who could ignore?

Timeless Waltz of the Ocean

The waves joined hands for a cheeky waltz,
With dolphins twirling, throwing their faults.
A narwhal in tights danced with delight,
While sea cucumbers grooved left and right!

Fish spun around in a sparkling rush,
Drumming on shells, oh the joyful hush!
Seahorses pranced with tails intertwined,
Making up steps that were one of a kind.

As waves rolled on, up and down, with glee,
The barnacles chimed in a sticky jubilee.
The shoreline giggled at the fishy flair,
While starfish clapped with their arms in the air.

Reflections of a Briny Song

A gull on a surfboard caught a quick breeze,
Wobbling and wobbling, begging to tease.
His flip-flops flopped as he sped down the crest,
"Surf's up!" he squawked, not caring for rest!

A crab with a mic took the spotlight,
Rapping his verses, oh, what a fright!
Clams snapped their shells in a clamorous cheer,
While fish played the beat—a catchy veneer!

But then came the octopus, slick and spry,
Dancing with arms that flailed up to the sky.
With twists and turns, he stole the show,
While the jellyfish swayed, putting on a glow.

Resonate of the Moonlit Bay

A seal with a hat took the stage,
Dancing with fish, a grand rampage.
With splashes and laughs, the night took flight,
Under the moon, what a silly sight!

Crabs in tuxedos joined the parade,
Pointing with pincers, they weren't afraid.
Jellyfish glowed like disco balls bright,
For a party of sea creatures, what pure delight!

Turtles rolled over with mischievous grace,
A conga line formed—oh, what a race!
The seaweed swayed to the quirky tune,
As clams clicked their shells under a big, round moon.